My dear friends,

Please forgive the flaws you may [illegible] book of affirmations. Because of th[illegible] live in at the moment and for the sa[illegible]ealth of all our neighbours and friends, I send this book out into the world naked and vulnerable. Without being able to receive a "Proof of Author's Copy" I release this book, mistakes and all, to the gentle hands of you, dear reader. I ask for your understanding. I did my best for the moment and when I become aware of the mistakes, I will do my best to correct them as soon as possible.

I ask for your kindness in this. I am just so excited to share this book with you. I sincerely hope that you all stay safe and healthy and live the most joyful life you can, even in these strange times.

Thank you,

Kim West

Book design by Walter Brunt

ISBN 978-1-9994668-9-3

This is dedicated to Kira - the Princess Puppy.
The bestest friend anyone could ever have.

What Kira Would Say to You

(If She Could)

A little book of joyful affirmations

Introduction

These are uncertain times.

There is so much pressure to be perfect, comparing ourselves to others.

We have all been there but each of us goes through these moments of up and down differently and no one formula works for all. It is not a one size fits all solution.

We all need someone who will just hold our hand, listen and keep watch while we rest.

Our cherished pets are good at just that. Not all of us are lucky enough to have a fuzzy friend by our side so for a moment I lend you mine, in spirit, anyway. This is Kira. She has brought so much joy into our home we often joke that she is an enlightened spirit. This thought got me thinking, what if she could talk? What if Kira- the princess puppy, could speak the lessons of joy we are all trying to understand. If she could, I bet these are some of the affirmations she would say.

These are words that, when spoken out loud to yourself, can help make big, joyful changes in your life. I, myself have often written these on my bathroom mirror so I can repeat these thoughts to myself as I get ready for the day. These words have helped me through dark times and lifted my spirits up even more during light times. Either way I was in higher spirits after telling myself these joyful thoughts. I hope that they help you as well get to that joyful place in your life.

About Kira - the Princess Puppy

Kira is a four year old beagle cross and she came into our lives on Valentine's Day 2016. Our home at the time was much too big for the two of us, rambling around the empty rooms, wondering what it was all about. We were in our early 40's and childless but had purchased a three bedroom rancher with the hopes of filling the space with pattering little feet. We got the home ready, did reno after reno, fixed up the yard and waited. Then realized that dream might not happen. We are very much of the mind that life is happening the way it should so even though month after month we were disappointed we also had faith that our life path might have something different in store for us. That is when we decided to get a dog. Don't get me wrong a puppy is not the same thing as a child, and we understood this. That being said, when Kira came she filled all the empty space in our home and hearts. She made us laugh each day with her antics. Her heart was so big that she helped us love each other even more. Kira is a sensitive, thoughtful, funny, playful friend and we are honoured that we get to be part of her family.

What Kira Would Say to You

(If She Could)

A little book of joyful affirmations

Joy flows through me.

I attract joy into my life.

I choose to be joyful.

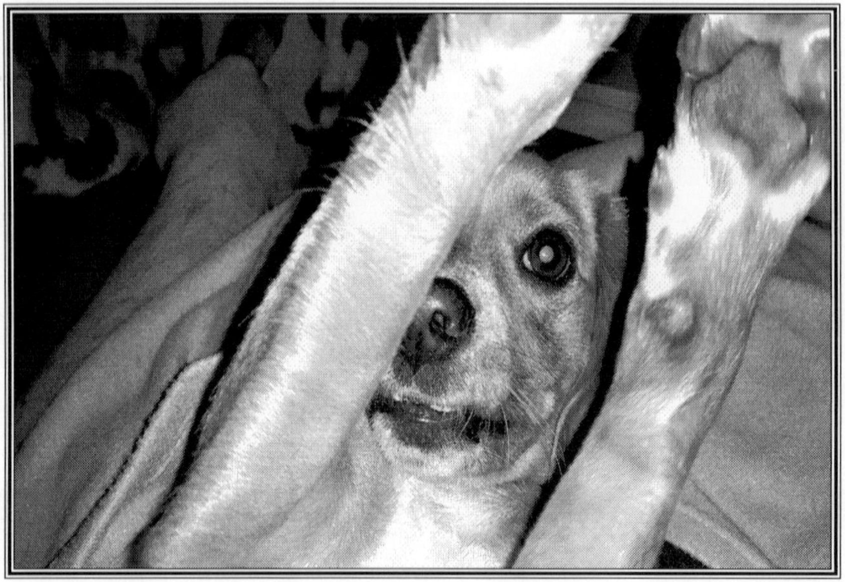

I look at the world with the eyes of joy.

Joy is in my heart and in my life.

I am joy.

I am willing to be joyful now.

I experience joy in everything I do.

I give myself permission to feel joy.

I am meant to live a joyful life.

I am joyful for all the wonderful things I already have in my life and those that are yet to come.

I am joyful for who I am and can be.

I am joyful for every gift that I’ve been given,
have now, and have yet to receive.

I am a living, breathing example of the joyful world I want to live in.

I am intentionally living a life filled with joy.

I am learning to live in joy.

Joy comes to me easily and effortlessly.

I am full of positive, joyful energy.

I welcome joy into my life.

I believe I can live a joyful life.

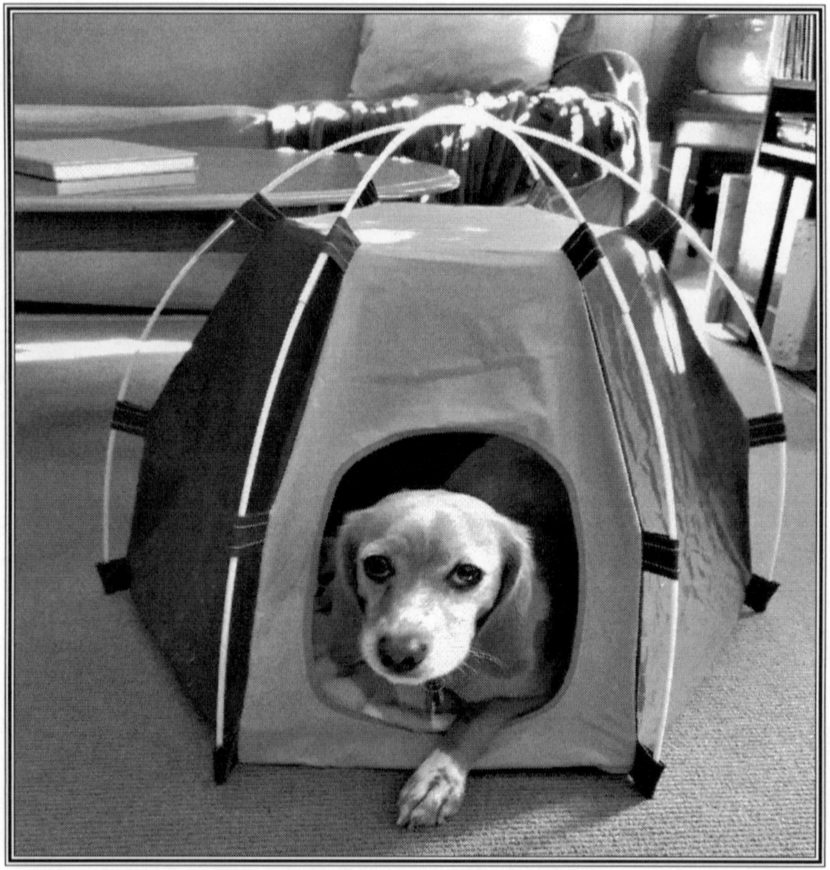

I deserve to be joyful and feel good.

It is my joy and pleasure to live another wonderful day.

Being joyful comes easily to me.

I know and accept the joy in myself.

I radiate joy and others reflect joy back to me.

Life is full of joy and I find it everywhere I go.

Every day of my life is filled with joy.

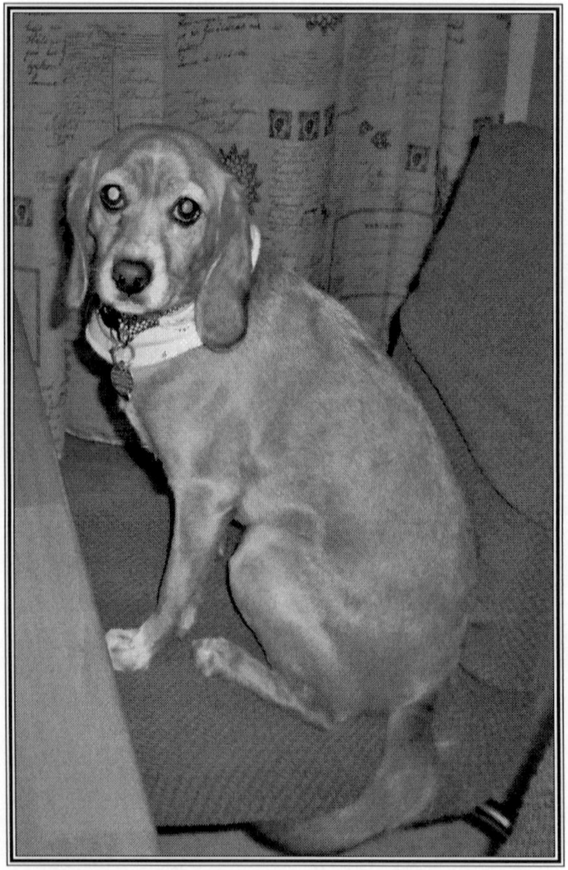

I wake up joyful and excited every day.

I find opportunities to be joyful everywhere I look.

My life is full of joy and magic.

I am surrounded by joyful people.

I am not afraid to express my feelings of joy.

I am a joyful being.

I am open and ready for all the joy in my life.

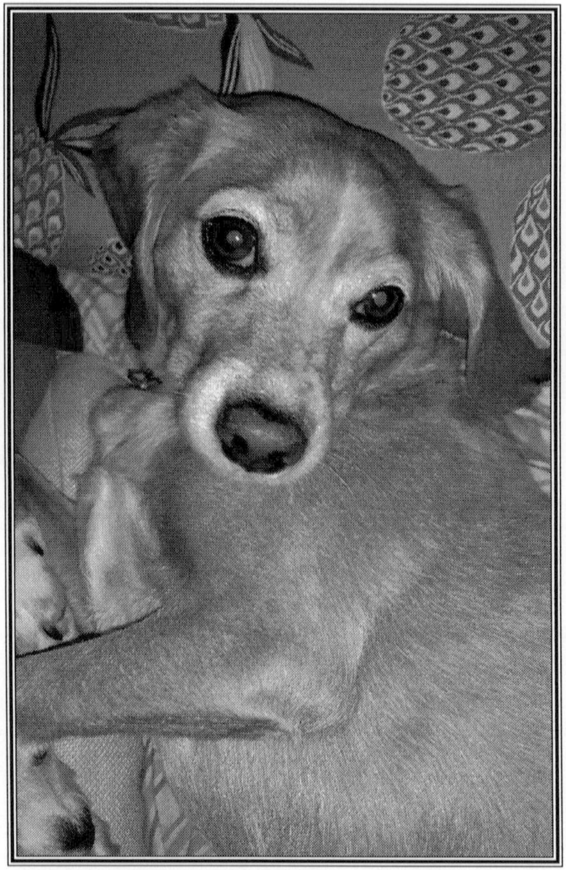

I am attracting joy into my life.

I am surrounded by endless joy.

I am filled with joy and peace.

I create a safe and secure space for myself
to feel joy wherever I am.

I use my time and talents to bring joy into my life
and the lives of others.

What Kira Would Say to You

I allow myself to be joyful without judgment.

I give myself the care and attention that I deserve,
so that I can feel joy more often.

I am learning valuable lessons about joy every day.

I am at peace with having joy in my life.

Every day I attract more and more joy into my life.

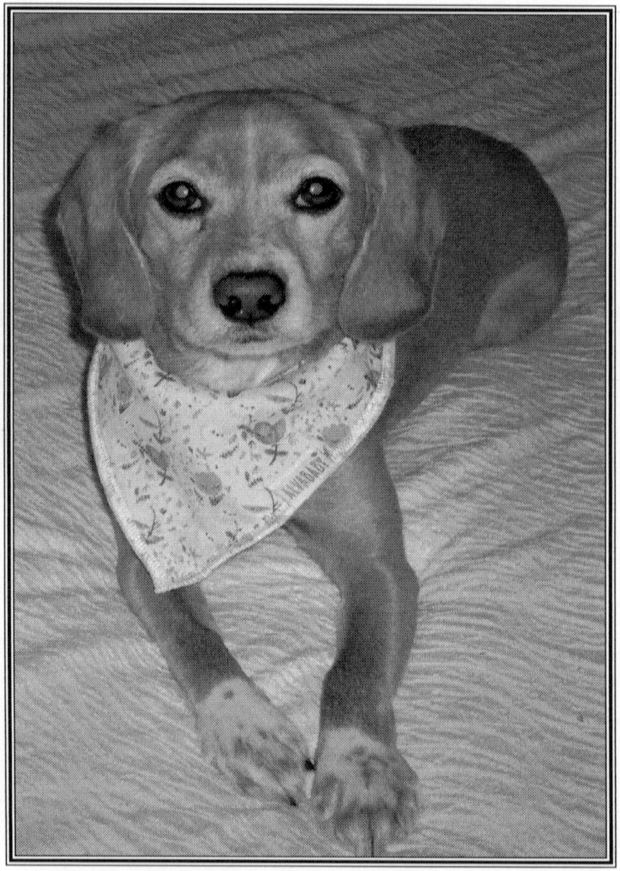

I have a joyful mindset.

I am free to be as joyful as I would like to be.

Joy comes to me daily.

Rabbit

Joy constantly flows into my life.

I have a joyful attitude.

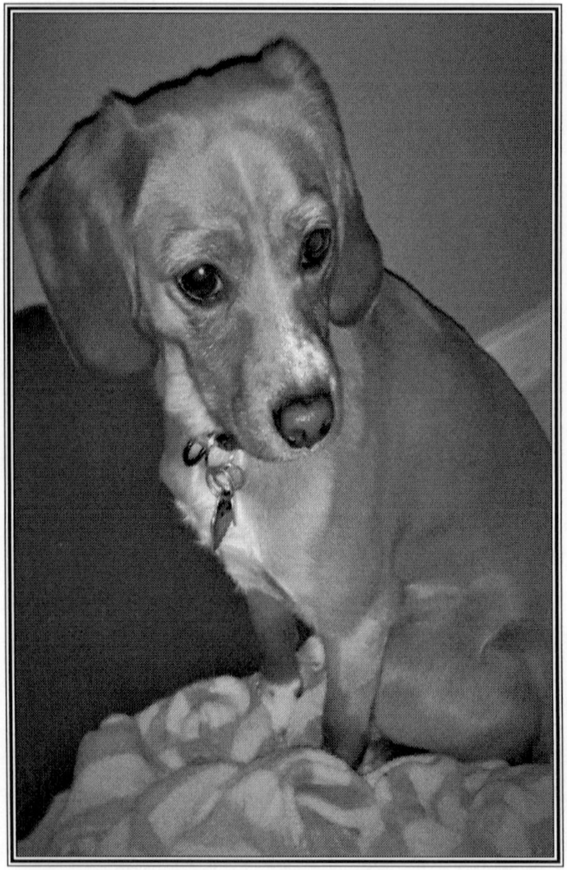

I am grateful for all the joyful moments
that I live in.

I release every block that held me back
from living in joy.

NOT ALL WHO
wander
ARE LOST

I only think thoughts of joy and well being.

About the Author

Kim West has been a Joy Coach running her own life coaching company "The Positive Path - A Journey Towards Joy-Joy Coaching" for many years doing workshops, seminars and personal coaching for the purpose of bring more positivity into our lives. Kim feels that in these times we can get bogged down with all that is negative in this world, where life becomes overwhelming and a struggle. She feels that it is important to see the positive in everyday moments and that there is more to life than just surviving the daily routine we entrench ourselves in. She reminds us of all that is good, positive and even joyful in our day to day living, helping us work toward a more balanced and happy lifestyle.

You can join her on Facebook @ Positive Path Joy Coaching.

Check out her first book, a small collection of phrases that gives a voice to your heart, "What Your Heart Would Say to You (if it could)" available on Amazon.

Manufactured by Amazon.ca
Bolton, ON

15126240R00072